MW00935461

Water Runs Red

water runs red
by jenna clare

WATER RUNS RED
ISBN: 9781793203144
Cover Design & Photo: Jenna Kilpinen
Torn Paper Photo: Jooinn
Watercolor Paper Background: PSD Graphics
Photo of Jenna on back cover: Aurora Phommalysack
Cover Handlettering: Margot Groner
Font: Walker Thin by Margot Groner
Printing: Kindle Direct Publishing
Formatting: Jenna Kilpinen
Copyright: 2019 Jenna Clare Kilpinen

Featuring photos by Jenna Kilpinen, Sophia Maxwell,
Aurora Phommalysack, Amy Schuh, Jessica Lewis,
Candace Kilpinen, Jon T. Kilpinen, Laura Gruszka,
Jacque Jordan, Jayda Iye Rust, Lexie Bluhm

for laura,
a shining supernova in a world of darkness

content warning:

depression/mental health issues
religion/Christianity/God
the colonization of america
blood/injury
asexuality
body image issues
ignorant old white men
toxic friendships
the devil
2016

table of contents:

prologue
prologue
prologue
prologue
prologue
prologue
prologue
prologue
prologue
prologue
prologue
prologue
prologue
prologue
prologue
prologue
prologue
prologue
prologue
prologue
prologue
prologue

prologue

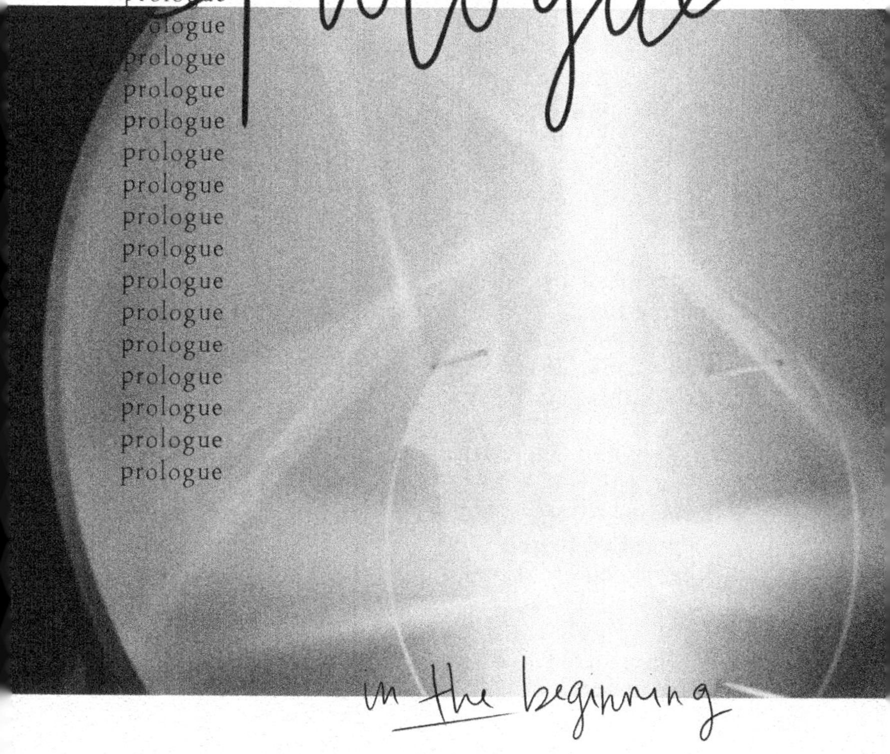

in the beginning

ANGER
HATRED
JEALOUSY

God held
all the power

in the beginning,
                man had a good heart,
                woman lived a safe life,
                God held all the power,
                and the devil appeared as a snake.

darkness curled around the body of man,
whispering lies
of self-loathing and hopelessness
until man could do nothing
but stew in his pain.

wickedness sank her teeth
into the flesh of man,
infecting him
with anger and hatred and jealousy,
until he turned on his neighbor.

and so, the poison followed
like a secret shadow,
cursing generations
and building empires
full of tyrant rulers.

the earth slowly evolved,
from man and woman
into fluid beings
who rejected the binary
of life and love
and sought revolution
for a brave new world.

an army of witches awakened,
in petticoats and pants,
in corsets and codpieces,
in platforms and penny-loafers,
and they rallied together
to find a cure
against the dying of the light.

that light lived inside every being,
an enduring glow that shined
as a beacon of goodness and truth.
while some chose to nurture
the power that gave them breath,
others still abandoned it
and ardently embraced the night.

landscape of nightmares

blackest sky loomed over the horizon,
promising a landscape of nightmares
as midnight settled over the land.
the earth beneath the feet of man
began to crack,
splintering under the weight
of a thousand broken cities.
and yet,
even as storm clouds gathered,
a new dawn prepared to rise.

a hero
a new dawn
RISES

they always warn you about the bad boys,
but what about the mean girls
who break your heart
and burn you at the stake?
— *the girl who cried witch*

prick prick prick
prick prick prick
prick prick prick
prick prick prick
prick prick prick
prick prick prick
prick prick prick
prick prick prick
prick prick prick
prick prick prick
prick prick prick
prick prick prick
prick prick prick
prick prick prick
prick prick prick
prick prick prick
prick prick prick
prick prick prick
prick prick prick
prick prick prick
prick prick prick
prick prick prick
prick prick prick
prick prick prick
prick prick prick
prick prick prick
prick prick prick
prick prick prick
prick prick prick
prick prick prick
prick prick prick
prick prick prick
prick prick prick
prick prick prick

Part I : Prick

i used to hear stories
of gallant princes
and the castles they ruled
in far off lands of magic,
so i kept searching
for a storybook fantasy
in my quiet reality.

*far off
land of
magic*

ruler of the innocent
lady of the lost souls
princess of the peasants

everywhere i went, i created queendoms.
i crowned myself ruler of the innocent,
lady of the lost souls, princess of the peasants.
my tiara had been woven out of flowers and fairytales,
my throne had been built out of daydreams and dimes,
and no matter who approached my castle gates,
i let them inside to join my celebration.
   — *i welcomed them to mine*
     because no one invited me to theirs

love with RECKLESS abandon

life flickers through my palace
as my bannerwomen come out of the shadows.
they awaken a spark in me,
raising my name and joining my coalition,
and even though i do not deserve
those fairies and sprites
who parade through my halls,
they love me anyway
with reckless abandon,
and i let myself enjoy their presence
as we belt out the anthems of our ancestors.
— *my special court*

at the brightest hour of the day,
a young enchantress broke through the clouds,
floating on feathered wings of freedom,
happening upon the tiny realm by chance.
plush contours of skin hugged her hips,
and a rainbow of ringlets rounded her cheeks.
she had escaped the phantoms of her past
the only way she knew how,
and now she longed for a new life to weave.
— *the collector*

after i built my own domain
out of words and paper and tape,
you and your wings knocked on my door,
offering me a grand feast and a sparkling crown.
you had claimed your own queendom,
you connoisseur of worlds,
and so your palace and mine sat side by side.
— *my first fairytale friend*

we were the same blood

your soul reflected mine
like a warped echo,
distant and ever-changing
but forever repeating
the same frequencies.

the two of us shared so much
that sometimes
i feared
we might morph
into the same not-so-perfect body.
— *fraternal friends*

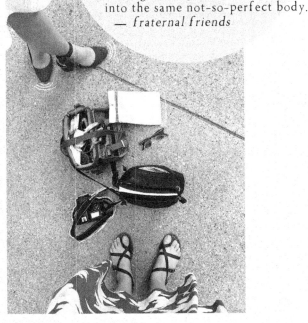

once upon a time
we were the *same blood*,
crafted out of the same symphonies,
destined to make the same mistakes,
walking the same path
until we decided to get lost
in opposite directions.
— *happily never after*

i pricked my finger
on your spinning wheel
and watched the world fade
until the only thing i knew
was you
  — *the curse of maleficent*

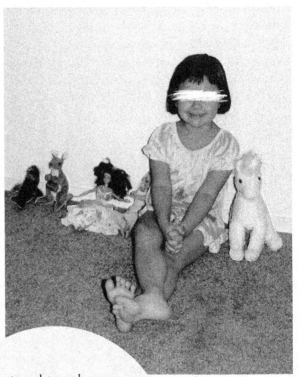

we reigned together
over the smallest kingdom
without gold in our pockets
or crowns on our heads,

but true wealth was no concern
because we found luxury
in the laughs we shared
and the stories we wrote together.

our lands held secret treasure troves
of soft-hearted animals and life-giving anthems,
and we tucked them into our souls
like they were precious jewels.

as long we had each other,
we did not mind our own lonely hearts.
we gorged ourselves on penniless delicacies,
and ruled our button-eyed subjects in peace.

FAT IS RADIANT FAT IS RADIANT
FAT IS RADIANT FAT IS RADIANT
FAT IS RADIANT FAT IS RADIANT
FAT IS RADIANT FAT IS RADIANT

when i looked at your curves,
i saw my own self reflected back at me,
and for once i didn't balk
at the excess life surging around my bones.
maybe we just have too much light inside us
to be contained by a small vessel.
— *fat is radiant*

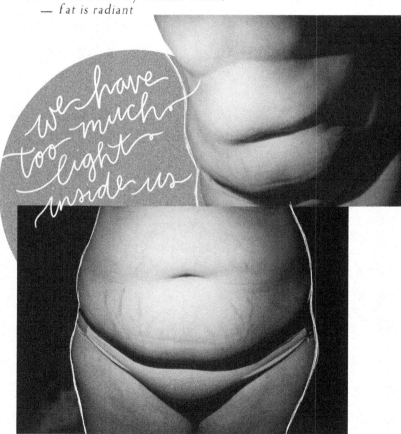

we have too much light inside us

i cemented myself to you
and your make-believe games
and your childhood dreams,
and your smile became
my second home.

i counted you as my first
— friendships mean just as much as romance

skeletons in the closet

when i asked about the skeletons
hidden deep within your closet,
you promised me
that they deserved their fates.
so i listened to your tales of woe
and added their names
to my list of traitors
without a second thought.

too cold
too loud
too much

after long days of laughter
and chasing stars across your painted sky,
we used to fall asleep
to the sound of the wind
as it tore through your bedroom
too cold
         too loud
              too much.
you didn't seem to notice
that it kept me wide awake
while your breathing slowed beside me.
— *i never understood your quirks*

the ~~the so~~ sound of the wind

friends can't be bought.

sometimes they can be bribed
with little kid luxuries,
like afternoon snacks
& only-child spoils.
— *the price was right*

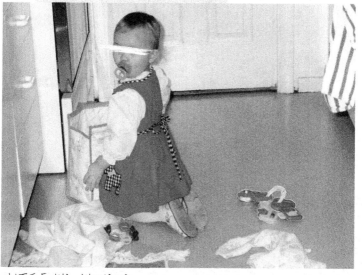

LITTLE KID LUXURIES

you always had a
Full House
no matter which game
we played
because you always
dealt
— *season 1 episode 13*

Monstrous,
self-obsessed
heart ♡

when our queendoms first joined,
i convinced myself that i had to be second-best
because of my monstrous, self-obsessed heart,
so i watched you dance on your pedestal
and allowed myself to sink even lower.

in time, i climbed up to join you,
fighting against the voices inside my head
until i could finally see myself
rise above the person i used to be,
and i thought you would be happy for me.

but you tried to push me,
crying sabotage and foul-play,
and i realized that your bubble gum tulle
masked the emerald villain
clawing its way up your throat.

what did you see
that made you so interested
in collecting me?
— *i wasn't limited edition*

i wasn't limited edition

maybe we didn't have as much
in common
as i once presumed
— *afterthought*

if i had been honest with myself,
i would have heard the devil
whispering in my ear
and tempting me
with my heart's dark desire
to reign over everything.
   — *"you're so much better than her"*

deep within
the branches of our family tree,
beyond our constitutional fathers
and melting-pot mothers,
our patriotic people are connected
by a line of disease
that plagues every household.
no matter how far we run,
we cannot escape
the fate of man,
so we turn to our many gods
and pray for salvation.
— *forbidden fruit*

we cannot escape the fate of man

man has every capability
of being good and just and true,
but instead of following the light
by making one difficult decision,
he spends his day
choosing darkness
ten thousand times
because he'd rather life be easy
than experience a single moment of discomfort.
— *the curse of man*

sometimes

d r
   i f
        t i
              n g

is worse than

fighting

city streets
stretch wider than mountains
and run deeper than oceans.
each block becomes
a not-so-perilous trek
that you deliberately avoid,
even when i beg you to find me.
— *i moved, but you stood still*

i studied your breathing
while we sat together,
but we built up walls
knowing the gates would never open
again.
— *the last time we spoke*

when you had finally collected
enough of this life that you had crafted,
you did what you always do
and flew away on gilded wings.
but as you ran off to the clouds,
i saw obsidian dripping from your shoes
and watched you transform
into the beast that had been hiding
beneath your skin.
— *true love doesn't exist*

the devil smirked
as she stole you away from me,
and i sat there
powerless.

for months i couldn't fall asleep
because of the bloodstained trees
that plagued my dreams
from birthday parties gone wrong.
the branches called to me through fuzzy tv screens,
ripping through my window like the winter wind,
watching patiently while i screamed for release.
so i turned on star-drenched lullabies
from the choirs of my youth
and disappeared into my mother's favorite song
until the only thing
haunting me
was your ghost.
   — *even then, the darkness whispered to me*

fire in my soul

strike a match on my ribs
until it starts a fire in my soul
so that my heart may become
a beacon of hope
in a body that is struggling
to see through the smoke
of temptation
— *prayer for inner darkness*

the whispers reached me
through grapevines
and behind backs,
and that's when i understood
you had left me behind.
— *sudden death*

the devil weaves empty promises,
calling out sweet nothings
to seduce her prey,
as if her hate could snuff out their fire.

this eternal shapeshifter of chaos
masquerades as many,
but at her core,
she is only the enemy of goodness.

many have tried to asphyxiate her
black tendrils of bitterness,
but she only burrows deeper,
biding her time.
— *a patient predator*

CHAOS CHAOS CHAOS CHAOS CHAOS CHAOS CHAOS CHAOS CHAOS CHAOS CHAOS CHAOS CHAOS CHAOS CHAOS CHAOS

you only returned once,
crashing into my castle
and smashing my storybook world to bits.
i watched you collect my own bannerwomen,
desperately trying to overthrow my rule,
but they did not abandon me so easily.
when you called for my demise,
each of my allies returned to my side,
and we barricaded the doors to shut you out.

   — *"once upon a dream"*

the poison of jealousy infected you,
a blackness darkening your veins,
and i couldn't stop the disease
until it was too late.

you shifted into a dragon,
breathing fire down my neck,
as if i was an entitled prince
storming your walls to defeat you.

but i couldn't save you from yourself,
and in the end, your blood ran green,
consuming you,
until i was forced to retreat.

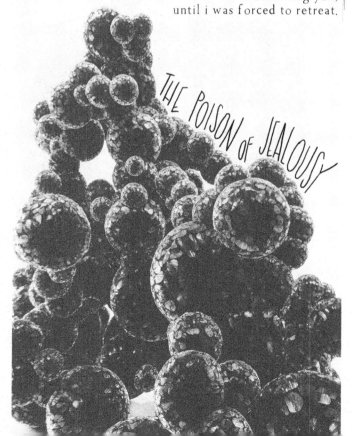

THE POISON of JEALOUSY

for so long i had watched the tyrants with disbelief,
never quite understanding their viciousness
as they hungered for power,

but now, with my palace threatened
by your jaded flames,
i see those villains in a different light.
— *"everybody wants to rule the world"*

with tea-filled harbors,
guns drawn,
eyes to the sky,

we swore that
no one
would rule us.

so instead,
we decided
to rule ourselves.

but in policing ourselves,
we became
our own dictators,

sending in battalions
to stuff one definition of love
down the throats

WE SWORE NO
ONE WOULD RULE US

of a people
who only seem to know
how to hate.

in order to win our democracy,
we sacrificed the light in our veins
and watched our leaders become rulers,
like the emperors of some infamous dynasty.
hatred sunk its teeth into this new-found dominion
until prejudice flooded the streets
and the people drowned themselves in darkness.
    — *the things we hid in museums*

our people raised a wall between us
and the rest of the world,
as if a few bricks could keep out the epidemic
that had already contaminated our leaders.
    — *history repeats itself*

the world fades to black and white,
creating colonizers inside shades of gray
until these men rule over their castles
like children who have not learned to share,
throwing tantrums
and stealing toys they don't even want.
— *conquerors of the playroom*

CHILDREN WHO HAVE NOT LEARNED TO SHARE

with careless ignorance and quiet greed,
the generations before us
set the world on fire.
so we inherited the chaos
without concern
because they taught us
"there is freedom
        in burning the words of anyone
                who disagrees with you."

— *legacy*

legacy

there is a shadow
contaminating the earth,
rising up after years
of covert destruction.
as soon as it infected you
and the beast within,
i watched the parasite
dig its nails
into every heart
and every headline
until all i could see
was black.
    — *the obsidian resurrection*

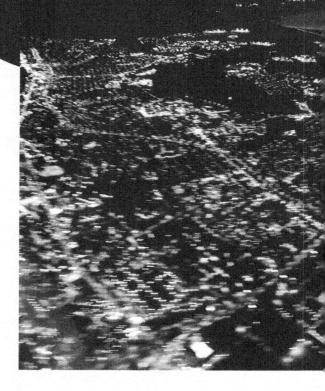

i have fought more difficult battles
than gunshots and sword-swipes.
i have seen more brutal defeats
than fallen armies and wounded warriors.
the real 'war to end all wars'
is waged on pillows and bedsheets,
against sharp edged thoughts,
in between the folds of the brain.
— *you joined the enemy and left me defenseless*

retreat

people slip through my fingers
like time
like the ocean
like the one that got away
— *i always let them go*

deep in the chambers of my heart,
i buried a secret so black
it stained my fingers
and clung to my clothes like smoke:

at my darkest,
i retreat
until even those closest to me
become my adversary.
— *making enemies of all*

i found myself
on my own,
lost in oz.

you used to have
my ruby slippers
until you gave them away.
— *i can't go home now*

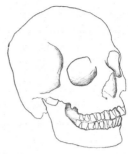

when you weren't looking,
my people told me to run.
they cried out warnings
because you drained the life
of those who crossed your path,
but i didn't listen.
— *the skeletons in your closet*

they cried out
warnings

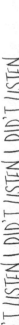

I DID'T LISTEN I DID'T LISTEN I DID'T LISTEN

i never meant to fight against you,
but you gave me no choice.

your deadly fire suffocated me
and forced me to build a barricade
of thorns around my heart.

so i drew my sword
and plunged it into your chest
to make sure you never hurt me again.

but in the end, your magic saved you,
and all i could do was weep for who we used to be.

after the smoke cleared
and your dragon disappeared,
i looked around
to see who i had forsaken
while i was busy plotting your demise.

rather than deserting me,
those forgotten friends
rallied behind my banner
and took up arms by my side
until i had the strength to rebuild.

forgotten friends

57

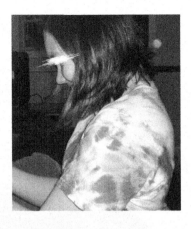

2009

the darkest time of my life
beats like an 808 drum,
incessantly hounding me until i break.
it curls around my tongue like key lime,
just sweet enough to savor,
but too tart to indulge.

the darkest time of my life
suffocates me like stubby green cotton,
rubbing against my skin
until long after the softness has faded.
it haunts me like old gum,
always popping up uninvited
and caressing me too intimately.
— *2009*

brain fog spreads like an epidemic,
preying on unsuspecting princesses
and attacking the subjects of their queendoms.

it appears out of nowhere,
a grim harbinger of nightmares to come,
and sentences its victims to a slow, painful death.

that ominous cloud has begun stalking me,
tormenting my thoughts
as i spiral deeper into myself.
  — i fear i may have been contaminated

i will never understand
how people survive
without faith
without grace to anchor them
without a god to save them.
not because religion is "right,"
but because it's so much easier
than facing the devil alone.

grace
TO ANCHOR

resentment hovered around me,
stifling my starry heart
and preying on my narcissistic soul,
but i forced myself
to bury you
so i could try to move on.
— *"you" has become "her"*

i saw sparks fly

once i closed the door
on my first fairytale friend,
i looked to the fiery women around me
to guide me back to my home.

even after i had set them aside,
their eyes still glowed with kindness.
when they came back to fight for my queendom,
i saw *sparks fly*.

i have seen witches hiding in the shadows,
and in their many faces, i see myself.
but even now, their magic eclipses mine,
bursting into the world like supernovas.

those enchanted beings gather in secret,
passing kisses and potions,
wishing away the entitled dogs
who treat them like pets.

so when i question my place
and wonder who i've become,
i let their smiles anchor me and remind me
that i am overflowing with potential.

even my bannerwomen couldn't save me

Scoured
pleaded
prayed

a new darkness sank its teeth
into my fractured heart,
and i searched frantically
for an antidote.

but the solution never came
even though i scoured
and pleaded
and prayed.

so i folded up within myself
and numbed my thoughts
instead of holding out hope
for a saving grace.

i sank into nothingness,
and even my bannerwomen
could not
save me.

they say you cannot
love someone else
without loving yourself
first,

but if we believe
our bodies are not entitled to love,
then how will we ever love ourselves
enough to love another soul?

love
yourself

i don't wanna kiss girls
i don't wanna kiss boys

what am i
what am i
what
am
i

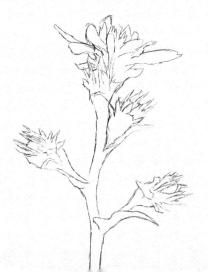

~~un de~~ im drowning in headlines

maybe i never noticed
the growing void inside my chest
because her sunshine shielded me
from the hopelessness of the world
— *drowning in headlines*

→ growing void

66

i built a blockade
around my castle
until even my mother
couldn't get in.

*build
bridges not
barriers*

who would we have been
if i hadn't wasted all that time
raising barriers
instead of building bridges?

~~wicked?~~
~~jealous?~~
both

sometimes i fear
my skin is turning green,
and i wonder if that is why
i don't like mirrors.
— *am i wicked or jealous or both?*

Part II BLEED

bleed bleed bleed
bleed bleed bleed
bleed bleed bleed
bleed bleed bleed
bleed bleed bleed
bleed bleed bleed
bleed bleed bleed
bleed bleed bleed
bleed bleed bleed
bleed bleed bleed
bleed bleed bleed
bleed bleed bleed
bleed bleed bleed
bleed bleed bleed
bleed bleed bleed
bleed bleed bleed
bleed bleed bleed
bleed bleed bleed
bleed bleed bleed
bleed bleed bleed
bleed bleed bleed
bleed bleed bleed
bleed bleed bleed

we are too preoccupied

the devil has made her empire
while the backs of the people are turned,
and they look the other way
out of ignorance and distraction.

she waits
until we are too preoccupied
with our own selfish lives
to strike.
— *misdirection*

i retreated further
into my palace of stone
and built a tower just for me
because creating something was easier
than venturing out into the world
of forced conversations

built a tower
just for me

KNIGHTING HERSELF

not so far off, in another land,
a dame strapped on her armor,
knighting herself
so she could fight her own wars.
with silver chainmail and a sword to match,
she hopped on her horse
and chased the stars.
her cavalry followed behind,
obeying her orders
and awaiting her visions
of the darkness to come.
— joan

when my sanctuary was complete,
i curled in on myself,
shutting out the world
because it didn't understand me
like i seemed to understand the people
within it.

but then one day you showed up,
with pink-streaked hair
and a shining suit of armor,
and you promised me a new start
because you once had a tower of your own.

for the first time in ages,
i forgot about the one who left me behind,
and i opened my gates to someone new,
a lady who saw me as i was,
who resonated with my brokenness.
— *my second fairytale friend*

you res you resonated with my brokenness

my second fairytale friend

my wickedness mirrored yours

though i tried to hide it,
you recognized my wickedness
because it mirrored your own.
so we overlooked our darkness
as if it did not matter,
and ran off
to have *one short day* together.

i should have known then.
— *green was your favorite color*

you remind me of *her*

.

.

.

i hope we get a different ending

we bonded over shattered hearts
and wounded self-esteem,
each of us lifting the other
until we finally made our souls whole.

our laughter united us,
stitched us back together,
and soon all my favorite moments
linked back to you.

our laughter united us

you and i have both been hurt
by the same types of people,
so we sentenced a decree
to silence all the turncoats
and banish their ghosts.
  — *the new ladies of the queendom*

a thousand constellations
lit up the sky above our heads,
and i felt the world spin on
without us.

so we laid there in the grass
with our heads side by side
and casually discussed death
as if it was the weather.
— *maybe we were depressed after all*

my forgotten friends, my bannerwomen,
watched me grip your hand
and descend into a sea of obsession.
in the thick of my fever dream,
i neglected the ones i claimed to love.

and as i receded once again,
dragging my new heroine into my soul,
i didn't notice the enemies of the light
scheming behind closed doors
and lining up their soldiers for bloodshed.
— *misdirection ii*

i receded once again

burrowing into their ignorance

the people had long since become comfortable,
burrowing into their ignorance
and forgetting the threat
that lay beneath the surface.

while the royals lounged in their privilege,
the creatures of the night feasted
on weak minds and empty pockets,
laying waste to those who could not protect themselves.

change does not often come
until God shatters the safety nets of the nobility,
and they are forced to live
like the ones they push to the side.

we both rejoiced
when you found your person,
a partner to fight by your side,
and he swept you off your feet.
he shined so bright
that i didn't even notice
his cunning smile
until he had dumped his toxins
down your throat.
— *your prince charming*

*eventually
he faded just
like all the
shiny pennies
do*

i didn't mind being left behind
because i knew you were happy
with your knight in shining armor,
and i always thought
true love made us into our best selves.
— *1 Corinthians 13:4-7*

we shared
a common thread
but neither of us noticed
as it slowly began to
u n r a v e l

my life became a countdown clock,
ticking away one TGIF at a time
because you convinced my brain
that the present could not fulfill me.

you pushed me to look ahead
because (y)our future was all that mattered,
and we both believed
we'd have a happy ending.

it wasn't until i watched you
walk towards the sunset without me
that i finally realized:
i had wished away my life to be by your side.
— *720 days*

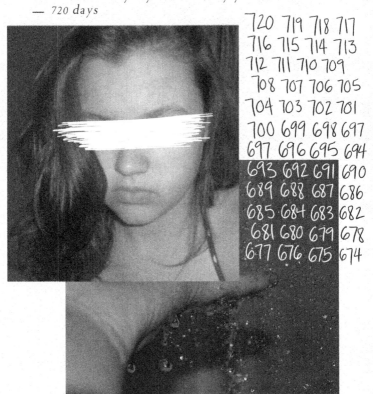

720 719 718 717
716 715 714 713
712 711 710 709
708 707 706 705
704 703 702 701
700 699 698 697
697 696 695 694
693 692 691 690
689 688 687 686
685 684 683 682
681 680 679 678
677 676 675 674

just because you don't remember to talk to me,
it doesn't mean i'm not here
— *the invisible girl*

invincible
not invisible

my biggest fear
is not spiders or death
or talking on the phone

it's that
you will call me
traitor
— *"dear john"*

please do not let our blood run cold
— *my secret prayer*

DO NOT LET OUR BLOOD RUN COLD
DO NOT LET OUR BLOOD RUN COLD
DO NOT LET OUR BLOOD RUN COLD
DO NOT LET OUR BLOOD RUN COLD
DO NOT LET OUR BLOOD RUN COLD
DO NOT LET OUR BLOOD RUN COLD
DO NOT LET OUR BLOOD RUN COLD
DO NOT LET OUR BLOOD RUN COLD
DO NOT LET OUR BLOOD RUN COLD

for a fleeting moment,
i notice the lights leave your eyes,
and you flicker out like a match,
morphing into a monster
i almost recognize from years ago,
from another fairytale with a tragic ending.

then the creature disappears,
and you return as if nothing has changed,
as if you were still the person i thought i knew.
so i brush it all off
like the first snowflakes
of an unexpected blizzard.

I NEVER SIGNED THIS CONTRACT!

x _____

you begin to schedule our meetings
into brief sessions
where we keep the minutes
and stay within our allotted time slot.

every time we talk
i eye the man next to you,
hoping that one day he won't show,
but he's always there, chained to your side.

you don't seem to notice
that you are now part of a packaged deal,
legally binding, TERMS AND CONDITIONS APPLY.
now we can't talk without your lawyer present.
— *i never signed this contract*

i never asked you for anything
but you kept taking from me anyway
— *the giving tree*

you turned me
against everyone else
because you were afraid
they would turn me
against you

at first
you sliced me
on accident,

and your words
sank deeper
than intended.

i noticed the cut
a few days later
scabbed and speckled.

it took me a moment
to remember
how it got there,

but then your voice
echoed in my head
and my stomach lurched.

i never
questioned
you

i never questioned you
because i thought we had
the *same blood*
— "which witch"

SAME BLOOD

YOU FORGOT ABOUT ME

i should have known
when they introduced him to you

i should have known
when you kept talking about him

i should have known
when you turned into "we"

i should have known
when you forgot about me

remember when we rode
33miles
just to see
your face light up
with happiness,
but you wouldn't
walk the extra mile
to see me?

apologize

by the time i realized
he was actually a parasite,
it was too late.
you had become his willing host,
and the only person who could save you
was yourself.
— *you let him infect you*

I WAS TOO LATE I WAS TOO LATE I WAS TOO LATE
I WAS TOO LATE I WAS TOO LATE I WAS TOO LATE
I WAS TOO LATE I WAS TOO LATE I WAS TOO LATE

when he showed up in your visions,
your dreams for the future,
he masked himself behind fantasies
and made you believe he was safe.
i watched you sacrifice your heart
so you wouldn't lose your head,
and somewhere along the way,
you sacrificed me too.
— *queen of hearts*

have you ever
seen a friendship
disappe
before your eyes?
— *abracadabra*

every time you promise

every time i believe you

and every
        single
              time
you send me the same message

— *"sorry, i have to see him"*

you are more addictive than cancelled plans
— *withdrawal*

as soon as he stole your heart,
he hid it away
and buried it
so i would never find it again.

the hunt drove me mad
because i wanted to rescue you,
to remind you who was the real thief,
but the affliction had already taken you.

instead of heeding my warnings,
you chose his vows
and cried witch,
striking a match on the kindling at my feet.

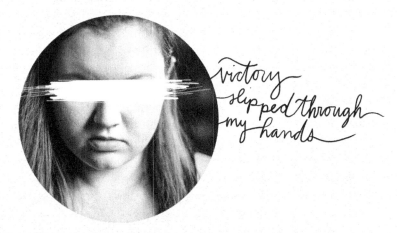

victory slipped through my hands

you gave me your shield for safekeeping,
offering another chance to win this war,
but victory slipped through my hands,
and i lost a moment in time
i couldn't get back.

when i tried to reason with you,
to explain the accident i hadn't planned,
you placed your sword on my neck
because at the end of the day,
you cared more about him than you did about me.
— *"off with her head!"*

you
told
him
to
speak
to
me
instead
of
doing
it
yourself

— *the closest i came to heartbreak*

i made excuses for you
i bent the rules for you
i broke myself for you

and what did it get me?
— *"you'll never understand"*

even when he stripped you of your armor
and transformed you into someone else,
you picked him instead of me.
— *what hurts the most*

*you picked
him instead of me*

NOT YOUR MAID OF HONOR

i should have let
someone else
throw you a pity party
— not your maid of honor

you morphed me into the Evil Queen,
forever commanding
my huntsmen,
        my necromancers,
                my magic,
to find your heart
so i could crush it
as payback
for all the pain you caused me.

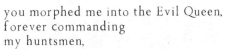

i've never been one
to burn bridges
but maybe
i'll douse yours
in gasoline
   — *the devil calls to me once more*

after months
of cold shoulders
and heartless hearsay,
the disease spread
until your hatred infected me, too.
— *welcome to the bad blood*

WELCOME TO
THE BAD BLOOD

Part III: STANCH

stanch stanch stanch
stanch stanch stanch
stanch stanch stanch
stanch stanch stanch
stanch stanch stanch
stanch stanch stanch
stanch stanch stanch
stanch stanch stanch
stanch stanch stanch

stanch stanch stanch
stanch stanch stanch
stanch stanch stanch
stanch stanch stanch
stanch stanch stanch
stanch stanch stanch
stanch stanch stanch
stanch stanch stanch
stanch stanch stanch
stanch stanch stanch

while the tyrants' power grew,
their empire fell victim to the pestilence.
just as infection spreads,
so do the ways of the wicked.
— *there's no vaccine for evil*

the old condemn the young
for demanding change,
and the young denounce the old
for keeping with tradition.

in an age of division,
the devil's job is easy,
for all she must do
is wait for chaos to breed.
— *generations of hatred*

age of division

you promised me once
that no matter where we ended up,
our relationship was a guarantee,
a safety deposit
that would always come back to me,
but i guess those were just empty words.

eventually we drifted out to sea,
and you began to swim out of reach.
i called your name,
but you didn't look back
as you swam off to your new kingdom
and left me floating alone on my raft.
— *one thread, and the whole world unravels*

Come back
to me

i couldn't imagine life
without you,
but now
i don't have to.
— *you imagined it for me*

each of our friends
allied with me,
and i watched your life
d i s i n t e g r a t e
before my eyes.

your downfall
still
did not
bring you
back to me.

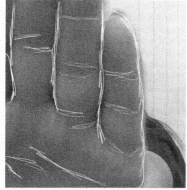

my mother asked
about you
only
once

and yet
somehow she knows
we no longer
speak

WE NO LONGER SPEAK
WE NO LONGER SPEAK
WE NO LONGER SPEAK
WE NO LONGER SPEAK
WE NO LONGER SPEAK
WE NO LONGER SPEAK
WE NO LONGER SPEAK
WE NO LONGER SPEAK
WE NO LONGER SPEAK

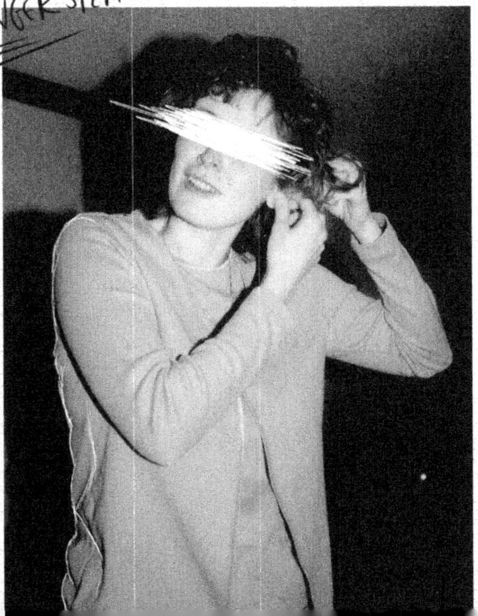

WATER RUNS RED

maybe they say
blood is thicker than water
because the water runs red
no matter what you do
— *there is always blood*

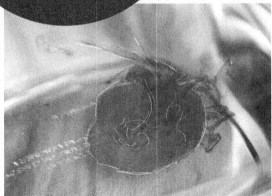

blood is thicker
than water

i keep falling into the same traps,
a relationship cycle that never changes,
different faces, same old game,
and when the chips are down,
i always lose.

waiting for the souls of kings

the devil gambles away her fortune,
losing frivolous evils and smaller discords
while she sets her eyes higher,
on a more satisfying prize.

instead of simple chaos,
this blasphemous goddess waits for the souls of kings,
planting her seeds of animosity and apathy
into the minds of bitter monarchs and wicked rulers.

she baits them with gold
because only the rich man is foolish enough
to condemn the world to poverty
while he sits alone on his throne.
   — *not a queen or a monster*

i am so sick
of watching allocishet white men
save the world.

it is the allocishet white men
we have to save the world
from.
— *the same old movies*

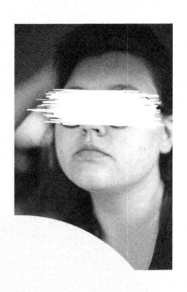

earthquakes rattle beneath our fingers
as a hundred different bombshells explode
across our tiny universe.
but we cannot stop the blows,
cannot shield our children,
and so we sit with tired eyes,
staring at nothing,
as we wait for the aftermath.
— *defeated rebels cannot fight back*

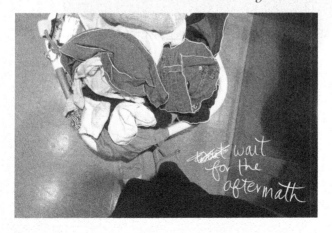

115

God's not the problem
it's His people
— *christianity is not always Christ*

HIS GLORY—

the church plays god
even as it claims
to fight for His glory,

but God does not
want this fight.
He only wants love.

God scrutinizes the devil
as her whispers tear the world apart.
although she does not raise a hand,
she plants her rotten seeds
into the heads of the humans
knowing they will grow into weeds of hatred.
The Creator does not strike against her
because He is our eternal father,
always giving us the freedom
to fight our own battles
and worship our own kings.
— *timshel*

TIMSHEL
TIMSHEL TIMSHEL TIM
TIMSHEL TIMSHEL SHEL
TIMSHEL TIMSHEL HEL
TIMSHEL TIMSHEL
TIMSHEL TIMSHEL TIMSHEL
TIMSHEL TIMSHEL TIMSHEL TIMSHEL TIMSHEL
TIMSHEL TIMSHEL TIMSHEL TIMSHEL TIMSHEL
TIMSHEL

no quick fix

resistance starts quietly
with whispered words and hushed tones,
telling anyone who will listen
that corruption has feasted on the realm.

there are no explosions of change,
no victorious cries for justice,
no quick-fix assassinations
to shock the world.

revolution is feeding the poor
and standing up for the innocent,
even when the enemy tries to convince you
that selfish is the status quo.

rebellion has humble beginnings
because it must be pure at heart
to create a better world
and succeed where all else has failed.
  — *there is no magic in insurgence*

as we slumber,
the great power inside each of us
carefully opens an eye,
waiting for the perfect moment
to drag us from sleep
and rally us for battle.
— *you should have burned us like you did our ancestors*

we didn't know
what we were destined to become
until we lost control
and our magic grew wings
in the wake of a thousand injustices
    — *the rise of the witches*

we may not have found our power at all
had the commanders not forced our hand
and angered our hearts
    — *we owe them nothing*

as i watch the world around me,
touching and kissing and consummating,
i realize that i am some kind of other.
this otherness is not necessarily wrong,
but i cannot shake the feeling
that i am something else entirely.
am i more monstress
than human,
or am i just a new breed?
   — *that sinking feeling*

what if my story
doesn't have a prince
charming

does that still make me
the princess?

the answer is yes

maybe if i
doodle hearts
in my
yearbook
around the photos
of all the
"cute" boys,
i'll finally
think
straight

~~if you don't know how to flirt~~
~~if you forced yourself to pick a crush~~
~~if you can't figure out who's good-looking~~
~~if you never think about undressing someone~~
~~if you cringe when people kiss~~

if you don't feel sexual attraction regularly or at all
— *you may be asexual*

"so who's your crush?"
can't you read my face
to see that question
crushing
me?

just because
i treat you like
a partner,
it doesn't mean
i want to
kiss you.
— *i fall in love all the time,*
just not like that

I want someone else too,
but not the someone else
who kisses me beneath
a sky of blue

12/20/2014

allosexual (adj)
sexual attraction
towards another
person

everything i see
invalidates my existence

i cannot relate to your reality
because it is not mine

stop forcing your allonormativity
d
    o
       w
          n
             my
                  throat

queer (*adj.*)
1. is not heterosexual
2. does not fit cultural norms of sexuality
3. can be a slur
4. represents a community
5. is being reclaimed
— *when will our asexuality be enough?*

our lack of sexual attraction means
we are not straight enough
our lack of overwhelming oppression means
we are not gay enough
— *square peg, round hole*

the otherness that clouds my veins
does not make me inherently wicked,
but i wonder if
because i am so different
from everyone i know

.
.
.

have i become the same
as any other wounded animal
that bites the hand of its owner?
— *did you contaminate me?*

Am I WICKED?
Am I WICKED?
Am I WICKED?
Am I WICKED?
AM I WICKED?
AM I WICKED?

the days grow darker

as the days grow darker
and a storm begins to materialize above,
the rebels hide in plain sight
to watch over the corrupted colony.

their magic must remain safe,
so they do nothing
as the innocent are lead
to the butcher's block.

WE SAVE OUR MAGIC
INSTEAD OF
OUR
PEOPLE

the less we do to help the helpless,
the more the darkness grows within us.
— *inaction only benefits the commander in chief*

the devil comes in many forms -
          the judging smirk of a stranger
          the narcissistic laugh of a friend
          the disappointed scowl of a reflection.
she feeds on you from within
and attacks you without.
and even though desolation stands in plain sight,
she often impersonates your deepest desire,
tempting you with perfection
and stealing away your heart
until your obsession consumes your whole self.
and after all the pain she's caused, she sits in the shadows
and comforts you with even more despair.
  — *darkness is the devil's daughter*

darkness

2am tragedies
piercing my insides

my thoughts are gunshots,
ringing out quick,
vicious, and unforgiving.

these bullets are 2am tragedies,
piercing through my insides
in a never-ending war against my own brain.

ceaseless shockwaves of destruction
echo through my mind,
whispering for me to raise a white flag.

but instead, i grip my blanket like a shield,
and i hope that sleep drags me under
while i stare at the ceiling.
— *insomnia*

insomnia

you do not visit me in my dreams,
so i savor the solitude
because it is the one place
your memory cannot touch me.

our lives diverged
as if two heartbeats fell out of sync
and i watchedwho i used to be
flatl i   n   e

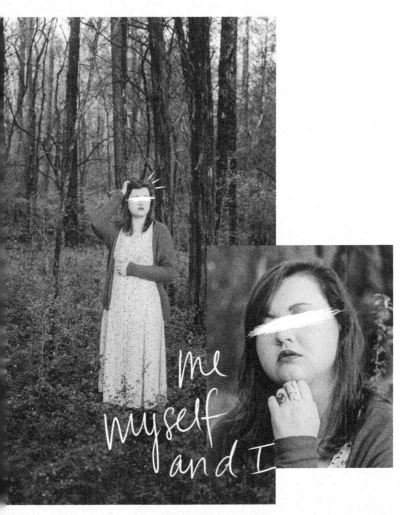

me
myself
and I

the war against myself began
without fanfare,
without declaration.
one day all was peace,
and the next day i was fighting for nothing.
 — *me vs. myself vs. i*

the devil preys on ruler and subject alike,
keeping both as her prisoners.
between the bars of their dark cells,
stranded within the vile bodies she has chained them to,
the captives writhe in agony,
unable to awaken from the horrors
of her ever-expanding queendom.
the world crumbles under her throne,
and she begins training the people of her army
to attack their unsuspecting allies
and eat their own hearts.
　　— *the tyrants' tyrant*

darkness and wickedness are sisters,
but not twins.

wickedness worships the devil
and spends her time stoking a jealous spark,
spawning greed and narcissism,
doing everything in her power
to snuff out hope.

darkness worships herself,
forever sulking in self-hatred,
bringing the world to its knees,
making truth believe
it should silence itself.
— *external versus internal*

almost almost
almost almost
almost almost
almost almost
almost almost
almost almost
almost almost
almost
ALMOST

in my head i have sent
a hundred letters,
each more malicious than the last,
each one meant to cut you
just as you cut me.
and yet,
whenever i try to speak to you,
to dial or not to dial,
i get lost in the words
i've built up like ramparts,
and hide behind my pride.
— *"i almost do"*

i apologize
for the words that slipped out

that wasn't me
that was the devil on my lips
— *it doesn't excuse me, but i'm still sorry*

I NEVER SAID A THING

i tried to tell you in person,
but you stopped seeing me.

i tried to call you,
but you must have gotten a new phone.

i tried to write you a letter,
but you probably wouldn't read it anyway.

in the end,
my words rusted
and i never said a thing.
— *how grudges begin*

my heart has never broken
from last kisses
or sappy love songs
or empty bed sheets.

instead,
it lurched,
sp   utt   er   ed,
                    s p i t,
and
s
            a
                n
                    k
to the bottom of the ocean
all because of
the bad blood.

so much
Bad Blood
Bad Blood Bad Blood
Bad Blood Bad Blood
Bad Blood Bad Blood
Bad Blood Bad Blood
Bad Blood Bad Blood

141

i stapled all my favorite song lyrics to you
until one day you stripped yourself from me.
you took all the good memories,
stole guitar solos, and pilfered piano motifs,
and you left me with minor scales and diminished chords.
i couldn't recognize the soundtrack of my life,
so i taped it back together with breakup songs.
— *now i hate putting on my headphones*

absolute nothingness
is preferable
to the kind of something
(or someone)
that makes you feel
alone

i wandered aimlessly
as i travelled along
a yellow brick road
on my own.
and i caught myself
turning a deeper shade of green.

I think I'm
a terrible person.

oh well.

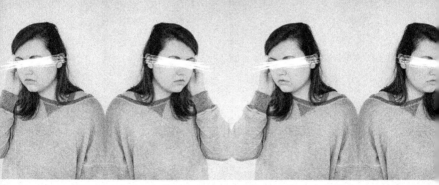

like all the infamous queens,
i drew my strength
from the misery of others,
and soon that misery
corrupted me too.
— *mirror, mirror*

hate latches on like a leech,
clinging to the bad thoughts
and provoking the despair within.

nothing can stop the blackness
from consuming her host,
so she feasts.

hate

i am so tired
of measuring my life in
people who have wronged me
— *your hate is my drug*

we must not characterize ourselves
by the lives we collect
because one day,
our treasure trove of compliments
and attention and conditional love
will catch fire
and leave us to burn.
— *children of dust and ashes*

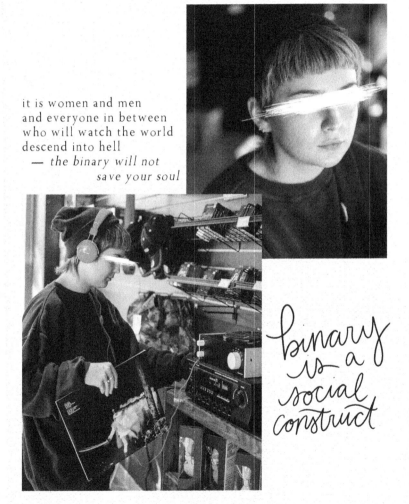

it is women and men
and everyone in between
who will watch the world
descend into hell
— *the binary will not
save your soul*

*binary
is a
social
construct*

the witches will rise

the old emperors
have reigned
too long.

we rage,
pleading for justice for our children,
but we are silenced, ignored, forgotten.

they call for us to burn,
but instead of cauterizing our indecency,
we shine brighter than stars.

we unite,
a coven of ethereal beauties
who have been overcoming obstacles since birth.

one day,
the tyrants will fall,
and the witches will rise.

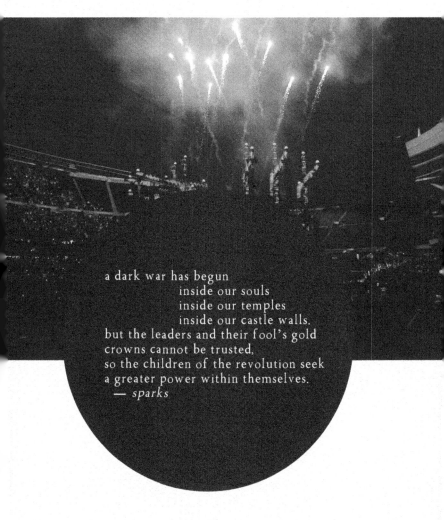

a dark war has begun
            inside our souls
            inside our temples
            inside our castle walls.
but the leaders and their fool's gold
crowns cannot be trusted,
so the children of the revolution seek
a greater power within themselves.
    — *sparks*

it's really late
think about.
~~it's when~~ ~~it's really~~ late
~~5/9/15~~ and think about
~~I must feel like to be~~ in love...
~~when it's really late~~
~~sit~~ ~~and think about~~ when it's really late
~~must feel like to sit and think~~ about
~~later I must~~ it must feel like to be in love...
~~5/9/15~~ ~~sometimes~~ when it's ~~really~~ late
in ~~I~~ like to sit and think about
~~it's what it~~ ~~must~~ feel like to be in love...
~~think about~~ sometimes 5/9/15 when it's really late
like to be in ~~like~~ to sit and think about
~~/9/15~~   what it must feel like to be in love...

                5/9/15
        sometimes when it's really late
         i like to sit and think about
         what it must feel like to be in love...
                5/9/15

no one ever taught me
how to
love
myself
    — *single & still learning*

in the months since you left,
my darkness multiplied,
and like a self-fulfilling prophecy,
i finally became the wicked witch
she once claimed i was
all those years ago.
   — *my spells are directed at you*

stitch stitch stitch
stitch stitch stitch
stitch stitch stitch
stitch stitch stitch
stitch stitch stitch
stitch stitch stitch
stitch stitch stitch
stitch stitch stitch
stitch stitch stitch
stitch stitch stitch
stitch stitch stitch
stitch stitch stitch
stitch stitch stitch
stitch stitch stitch
stitch stitch stitch
stitch stitch stitch
stitch stitch stitch
stitch stitch stitch
stitch stitch stitch
stitch stitch stitch
stitch stitch stitch
stitch stitch stitch
stitch stitch stitch
stitch stitch stitch

Part IV: STITCH

i try to spin
the green in my veins
into seas of gold,
but the monsters cry out to me
beneath the waves,
and i cannot let them go.

i drown myself
in what-ifs and sour daydreams
until i cannot see the light
at the end of the tunnel,
and i wonder if i am destined
to sink to the *bottom of the ocean*.

i force myself
to breathe breathe breathe
as the deep dark blue
attempts to suffocate me,
and for a moment, i forget
the pressure building behind my eyes.

as i burrow deeper into myself,
i embrace my self-appointed prison.
the bubble around me compresses,
and it silences the voices of the queendom beyond
until all i can hear is my quiet breathing.
    — _no one can find me here_

i keep the bad blood
because it's
all i have left of you
— *grudges*

again & again & again
& again & again & again
& again & again & again
& again & again & again
again & again & again
& again & again & again
& again & again & again
& again & again & again
again & again & again
& again & again & again
& again & again & again
& again & again & again
again & again & again
& again & again & again
& again & again & again
& again & again & again

you
are the scab
i picked at
again and again
until you left
a scar

we have become so sidetracked
by the monarchs
who gorge themselves
on their fatal feasts of foolisness,
that we have failed to see the devil
and her children

d

r

i

p

their poison
into our half-empty cups.
— *misdirection iii*

i sit alone in my tower
watching the clouds
as they grow darker and darker,
and i sip from my emerald goblet
in stormy silence.
    — *i hope it's raining wherever you are*

do you wish
you had stayed?

red rivulets run
down the tyrants' gilded ivory thrones
as the blackness stains the republic
with innocent blood.
the youth fall
victim to that dark legion,
sacrificing the stars in their eyes
for a meaningless cause,
and their names are scrawled
across the streets like warning signs.
so each man prays for a savior,
pretending he wants change
for a system he's rigged in his favor,
but he's already saved himself,
so he chooses his comfort
over our survival.
   — *the most dangerous rulers Never Reign Alone*

i ripped off the gauze
too soon
too fresh
too painful,
but i wanted to see
what remained
after our stitches
pulled apart.

"well, now she's my ex-best friend."
— a breakup between friends is still a breakup

I CANNOT
TURN AWAY

there's an empty space
in my conversations
because your memory
keeps showing up
uninvited,
and i cannot turn away
your ghost.

i keep finding pieces of you
wedged in my pockets.
like the melody in my head
or the hair on my sleeve,
you are the *boomerang*
that won't leave me alone.

163

you can
         block me
         ignore me
         disown me
but i promise
you will never
         forget me
— *sincerely, the person who photographed your engagement*

i hope that one day
when i hear that song,
i remember
who i became
instead of
where you left me.
— *"wanted you more"*

who am
i
becoming

you must
find it in
yourself to be
more than what
people say...

the months without you
almost made me forget
all the hurt
you and your wicked prince caused me,
so i pushed against the door
and locked you both out of my head.
— *"you" has become "her" ii*

in the depths of my fortress,
i watched the world move on
without me,
and i feared
no one would find me,
even as i hid myself away.
— *i am my own evil stepmother*

my own evil stepmother

i found my comfort
in far-off places
and impossible worlds
because i hoped
that the magic would
l
  e
    a
      k
out of my head
and into my life

BOOKS
ARE
MAGIC

the men in power taught us
to be children of the revolution
long before they created their empire
of xenomisia.

with their greed-polluted minds,
the old-fashioned conquerors did not recognize
when they slipped us an antidote
and unknowingly aided in their own destruction.
— *books are our best weapons*

nothing has made me feel more alive
than sitting still
and being transported
to a new world
— *you are found*

i became so caught up
in the happenings of my own head
that i didn't notice
my fellow colonists burning all the witches.

even though i could avoid the stake,
i did not stop to think
of all the others who begged for my help
and watched me push them aside.
— *white feminism*

SOLITUDE

no one reprimanded me
for hiding in my castle of silence.
instead,
the women of my court
left me to my own devices
and allowed me to embrace my solitude.

i called on each of those enchantresses
when i couldn't stand my own reflection,
and they offered me pieces of their hearts
— a soft smile, a gentle hand, a listening ear —
and i took their strength
because i did not have any of my own.

it had to be you

sometimes your *cure* finds you
when you least expect it

light

light began all at once,
existing outside of time and space
and igniting the world
in one instant.

it never abandoned us,
though we have tried to ignore it,
though we have hidden from it,
though we have embraced the clutches of evil.

even as we reign in our own hell,
the beacon of love always welcomes us
back with open arms,
like a true, unconditional Father.

a supernova shimmered through the sky,
lighting up the cosmos for an instant,
and that explosion of space breathed magic
into the heart of a lost star.

the star cried out
as she saw the dark path laid out before her,
twisting in the sky to escape
her brutal, undiscovered destiny.

so she fell.
she hurtled to the earth,
clutching her inner spark like a talisman,
and for a moment she wondered who she'd be.

she awoke on the hard ground,
born of stardust and moonshine,
bright and flushed and breathtaking,
ready to set the world on fire.
    — *you are so different from the other two*

i watched the *Shooting Star*
tumble down to earth,
falling from grace
and shattering upon impact.
after she reknit her bones
and formed a new body
to contain her luminous self,
she picked herself up,
dusted off her boots,
and smoothed down her curls.
    — *i wonder if she'll stay*

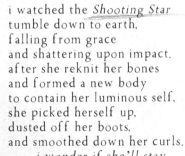

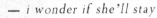

create untold worlds

fated to create untold worlds
and fight against an army of nightmares,
the starry-eyed sorceress arose from the dusted crater.
she left a trail of stories in her wake
as she looked for a new home
and breathed in the universe.

the creatures of the night watched her
while she honed her craft,
waiting for the proper moment to strike.
but the sorceress felt their haunting eyes on her back,
so she ran until her lungs gave out
and she ignored the prophecies that followed behind her.
— *"treasure can be salvaged from a sunken ship"*

i ran away from home
because i didn't want to cross paths
with all the ghosts i used to know
— *449 miles*

we finally found each other
after months of seeking some great perhaps.
fate pulled our strings
like puppets in a grand show,
until we collided
and our constellations exploded
into daydreams and secret wishes and silent prayers.
and for the first time in both of our eternities,
we found a missing piece
that fit both our puzzles perfectly.
  — *perhaps that something was actually someone*

the sorceress weaves magic
into the fabric of her clothes,
sewing sunlight into rainbows
even when she is shrouded in obsidian.
and in her eyes i see a thousand stars,
each guiding her on
to some great cosmic adventure.
  — *my third and final fairytale friend*

in months past, i'd become weary
of skeletons and dark secrets,
always apprehensive
my trust would haunt me,
always afraid i would love too blindly.

you housed a different kind of darkness,
a blue so deep that nothing would tame it.
that cloud hid within plain sight,
slowly consuming your heart,
never satisfied, never fulfilled.

and even though i saw those shadows
peeking over your shoulder,
i didn't fear them
because i knew they were merely a part of you,
like your unmanageable mane.

a blue so deep

third time's the charm
— *we are truly the same _blood_*

you never wake up before noon
you never go to bed before midnight
you always read the last page first
you hate portraits of yourself
you cast spells in your underwear
— *i always understood your quirks*

i think i loved you so much
because i saw myself in you

i think i loved you so much
because you saw me too
    — *abigail to my taylor*

I MISS WHO WE USED TO BE
I MISS WHO WE USED TO BE
I MISS WHO WE USED TO BE
I MISS WHO WE USED TO BE
I MISS WHO WE USED TO BE
I MISS WHO WE USED TO BE
I MISS WHO WE USED TO BE

you taught me how
to forge my own rose-colored worlds
out of paper and ink
because you cared enough
to want to visit the planets in my head

we didn't know
where we were going,
but that didn't matter
because we had each other.
— we were lost but "i miss those days"

your shining light crossed my path
before the monsters did,
but before we could make it to safety
they captured you instead.
  — *eventually the monsters found me too*

you disappeared beneath the waves
you disappeared beneath the waves
you disappeared beneath the waves
you disappeared beneath the waves
you disappeared beneath the waves
you disappeared beneath the waves

the obsidian parasite
wrapped her arms around your neck
and sang you a siren lullaby
until you disappeared beneath the waves.

i did not dive in after you,
fearing the creature would take me too,
and so i vowed to keep a vigil
as i waited for you to resurface.

you struck a bargain with the beast,
exchanging the glow in your eyes
for a couple more heartbeats.

after all,
she forced your hand.
you didn't have a choice.

*loved ones
become ghosts*

i have seen relationships crumble
and disappear without a trace,
but there is nothing more terrifying
than watching loved ones become ghosts.
— *is this how my mother feels?*

as i watched the cobalt shadow
devour the starlight inside you,
i felt you slipping away from me,
walking towards a course i couldn't follow.

i called out your name,
anchoring you in place,
but you just pulled your magic close
and faded into nothingness.

silence is everything

i tried
for so long
to make you talk to me,
but as it turns out,
we don't need to say a word.
— *silence speaks louder*

your scars
outnumber mine
and even though i try,
i will never quite understand
your sapphire void.
— *that doesn't mean i can't love you*

surely I
wouldn't be alive
if I weren't
worth something
7/1/12

we tiptoe into unassuming silences,
allowing each other to merely exist,
not asking for words,
not asking for answers,
not asking for anything
but a moment in time
where we can breathe together.

TOGETHER

i cannot bear
to see you
hate
my favorite person
in all the universe
when you look
in the mirror
   — *you are more than a pretty face*

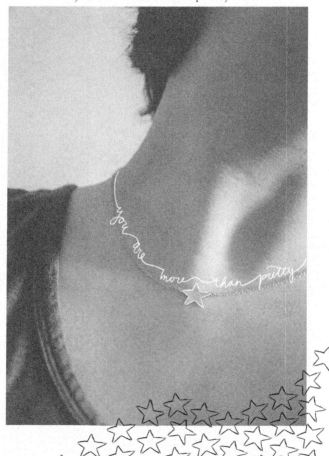

there is bravery in waking up
when corruption has morphed
our world into a nightmare.

for even when we cannot see it,
the light is rising up
R E S I S T I N G
the creatures of chaos.

there is starlight rippling through your veins,
fighting to keep your *head above water*,
even when you try to drown yourself.
and i hope one day, you will see the world like i do.
— *i hope one day, you will see yourself like i do*

your darkness
complements
mine
but we are both trying
to overcome
— *our inner demons*

i didn't know back then,
but i should have been looking for
someone who could teach me
about the magic inside myself
instead of someone who used my magic
for their own selfish schemes.
— *build me up, break me down*

there is no cure for the darkness,
only uncertain remedies and sometimes solutions.
in order to come back from the depths,
we must fight our own battles like soldiers
and i g n i t e the flames in our blood.
— *what they don't tell you*

i washed my hands
of the *bad blood*
but it kept coming back
— *dear lady macbeth*

i thought i'd learned my lesson,
but i keep scratching the same scars
over and over
and over again
until they're raw.
    — *did you break down the door,
            or did i let you back in?*

the green devil

the damage you and your prince caused
has buried my first heartbreak,
and now i have forgotten her face.

it is only you who visits me in memories,
but i tell you i've moved on,
and show off your replacement.
    — *the green devil resurfaces*

i felt
wicked

on my darkest days,
i sometimes wish
you would come crawling back
and give me an apology,
just so i could remind you
that you never accepted mine.
— *the first time i felt wicked*

you made me think
that i could only have
one
best friend,
but true friends
do not
hide you away
and keep you
from people you love.

true friends

darkest azure within
and wicked jade without
has turned our earth
into a battlefield

but instead of raising
our white flags
we clutch our black guns
until we are our own worst enemy

i knew i had darkness in me
i just never thought i could be wicked
— *i don't know how to stop*

the people that leave
force us to face ourselves,
even when we loathe
our own reflections.

we must become
our own partners in crime
against the devil herself
as she whispers
"you are nothing."

she isolates us,
casts us aside,
tears us away from our allies,
and seduces us with a black void.

but she cannot win
if we continue to resist,
and the best soldiers fight
with their own blood
glistening across their bodies.

I AM NOT NOTHING
I AM NOT NOTHING
I AM NOT NOTHING
I AM NOT NOTHING
I AM NOT NOTHING
I AM NOT NOTHING
I AM NOT NOTHING
I AM NOT NOTHING
I AM NOT NOTHING
I AM NOT NOTHING

stains
fade like
all scars
do

the nightmares still follow you,
my gentle sorceress,
like a spot on your soul
that will never disappear,
no matter how hard you scrub.
but eventually stains fade
like all scars do,
and now they are only a reminder
of the fires you crawled through.

in order to draw out the midnight
that has defiled my veins,
i cradle a glow of starlight
as it kisses my face,
until i am as brilliant as the moon.

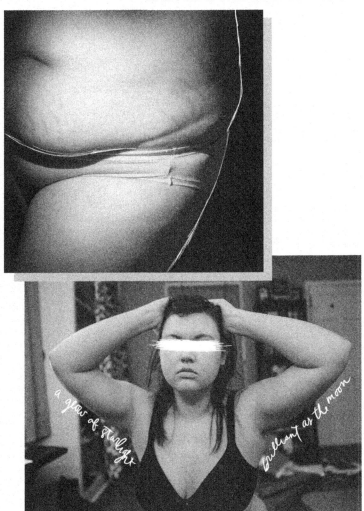

a glow of starlight

brilliant as the moon

you walked this road before me,
leading the way with breadcrumbs,
preparing me for the devastation ahead.

even though i followed in your footsteps,
we took different paths,
and soon i was lost in the winding woods.

i thought that i could save myself,
overcome the ghosts that watched over me.
i thought that i would be better on my own.

but i'm weak.
but i'm weak.
but i'm weak.

the dragons in my head weren't so big
as the demons and beasts that hunted you,
but i'm *weak*, and i couldn't fight them alone.

so you held my hand,
and combined our powers
until the world exploded into light.

as we rejoined the world of the living,
drinking in the sunshine
and vowing to rise above ourselves,
we heard the screaming
as the devil closed in on her prey.
— *november 8, 2016*

NOV 8, 2016
NOV 8, 2016
NOV 8, 2016
NOV 8, 2016
NOV 8, 2016
NOV 8, 2016

you stared at me, blinking back tears,
and we decided to split up our magic,
to assemble our separate armies,
to embrace our separate destinies
so we might make a difference
as individuals.
— *never forget, never regret*

SEPARATE ARMIES
SEPARATE DESTINIES

*embrace
your own
future*

sometimes in order to evolve,
we have to leave the ones we love
and walk alone for a time.

we do not abandon them,
we do not leave forever,
but we must embrace our own future.

they say distance is good,
that it makes the heart stronger,
so we give ourselves room to grow.

as each of us takes a different road,
we must remember to let go,
to give out freedom like confetti.

we don't have to chain people down
and hoard them like gold,
for if the love is true, they'll always come back.
  — *"i will see you again"*

I AM REBUILDING MYSELF
I AM REBUILDING MYSELF
I AM REBUILDING MYSELF

as i made a new home
and rebuilt my castle on my own,
i found myself becoming
stronger.

my magic awoke,
and i found a voice
that had once been forgotten
and lost in the shadows.

i joined the rioters
as they rallied in the streets
because so many people stood aside
and watched
while the leaders did nothing
    — *there is power inside all of us*

*we rally,
marching in
the streets*

thoughts and prayers are not enough

the witches were born
in classroom catastrophes
and rainbow nightclubs.
they were baptized in the tragedies
of a hundred roadside memorials
and a thousand unnecessary funerals.
as the rest of the world prayed
for a savior,
a second chance,
a rebirth for their nation,
the children of the revolution
A W O K E
and sharpened their words
to fight for those they lost
in the fires.

— *las vegas*	— *red lake*	— *tyrone*
— *orlando*	— *waddell*	— *aurora, co*
— *virginia tech*	— *jacksonville*	— *marysville*
— *sutherland springs*	— *seal beach*	— *spring*
— *killeen*	— *manchester*	— *isla vista*
— *san ysidro*	— *appomattox*	— *overland park*
— *austin*	— *carthage*	— *saylorsburg*
— *parkland*	— *omaha*	— *hialeah*
— *san bernardino*	— *san franscisco*	— *santa monica*
— *edmond*	— *louisville*	— *south valley*
— *fort hood*	— *miami*	— *sandy hook*
— *binghampton*	— *aurora, il*	— *grand rapids*
— *columbine*	— *sebring*	— *oak creek*
— *wah mee*	— *pittsburgh*	— *tucson*
— *wilkes-barre*	— *annapolis*	— *umpqua*
— *camden*	— *scottsdale*	— *carson city*
— *thousand oaks*	— *nashville*	— *st. louis*
— *wash. navy yard*	— *tehama county*	— *dekalb*

brokenness is our strength

sometimes witches speak
and the world refuses to listen,
so we string our words into songs
until our struggles become anthems
and our brokenness becomes our strength.
— *red lips and a mosaic heart*

211

the republic indoctrinated their people
with the myth
that loving another person
must break you
and remake you
into the image
of who they want you to be.

but the youth know a secret,
buried by those villains,
that loving other people
should cure you
and reassure you
that who you are
will always be more than enough.

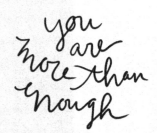

you are more than enough

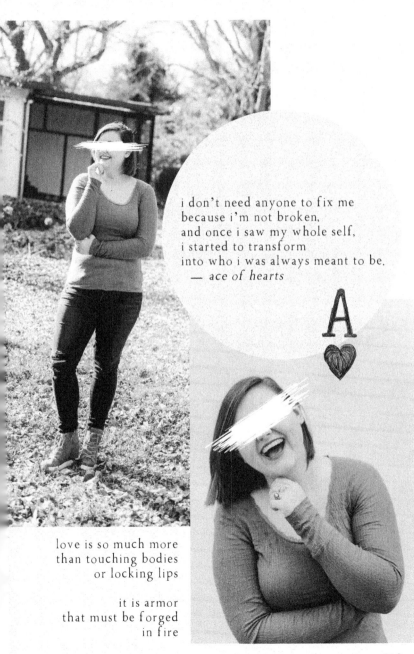

i don't need anyone to fix me
because i'm not broken,
and once i saw my whole self,
i started to transform
into who i was always meant to be.
— *ace of hearts*

love is so much more
than touching bodies
or locking lips

it is armor
that must be forged
in fire

213

people like paintings

i stare at people like paintings,
each with their own color palettes
and sweeping brush strokes.

the longer i watch them,
the more i wish
i could understand them.
— *aesthetic attraction*

there's nothing wrong with you
if you do not want
to see naked bodies

there's nothing wrong with you
if you do not want
to fall in love

there's nothing wrong with you
if you do not want

to hold hands
to kiss
to touch
to cuddle
to breed
— *there's nothing wrong with you*

THERE IS NOTHING WRONG WITH YOU

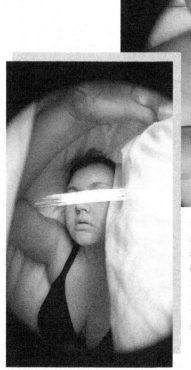

the worst kinds of wickedness
are the spells we cast
against
our own bodies
for nothing
is more deadly
than
self-loathing

FEAR
ME

for the first time,
i see who i have truly become,
and i'm not afraid of my scars.
— *the devil's worst nightmare*

I am the Guardian of my own Galaxy

i am so much more
than they ever painted me to be.

though my skin may be tinted green,
now it does not define me.

maybe that is why i start to stare
at the face in the mirror.

because now i see the vibrance,
and i want to stop hiding it.
— *for gamora*

217

even evil queens
can learn to forgive,
but i fear
that you never will.
— *wicked always wins*

S3E12

isn't there something romantic about friendship?

real love doesn't leave you bruised

or cut
or bandaged
or sore.

it builds you up
and gives you strength.
it is *the cure*.

i always thought
i should keep this magic
bottled up
and buried inside me,
but then i wondered,
what if i shared it?
— *the tyrant's worst nightmare*

please don't hoard your magic

LIBERATION TASTES SO SWEET

when i finally left my tower,
i was welcomed into a new family
by a court of women who shined
with overwhelming selflessness.

they didn't care about old legends
or whispers from years passed.
all that mattered to them
was that i felt safe.

and in that sisterhood,
i allowed myself to breathe
and center my life
on something new.
    — *the light i once feared*

i have never seen more magic
than when love is baked in an oven
and sprinkled with sugar on top
— *"what baking can do"*

chocolate banana PIE

even when i did not want to be found,
those enchanting women pursued me anyway.

they pushed me
to become fearless,
to use my conjuring for good,
even as the void gripped me.

so whenever i felt that dark cloud,
i clung to the ones who saw the light in me.

my north star

on the days i cannot
find my strength within,
i draw my power
from those who illuminate
the night sky
and lead the way like lanterns,
even as they are struggling
to keep their own heads above water.
— *my north star*

i don't deserve
your goodness

single single

i have been learning
how to love
myself

even as i try
to devour
myself
— *single*

Part V: SCAR

scar scar scar
scar scar scar
scar scar scar
scar scar scar
scar scar scar
scar scar scar
scar scar scar
scar scar scar
scar scar scar
scar scar scar
scar scar scar
scar scar scar
scar scar scar
scar scar scar
scar scar scar

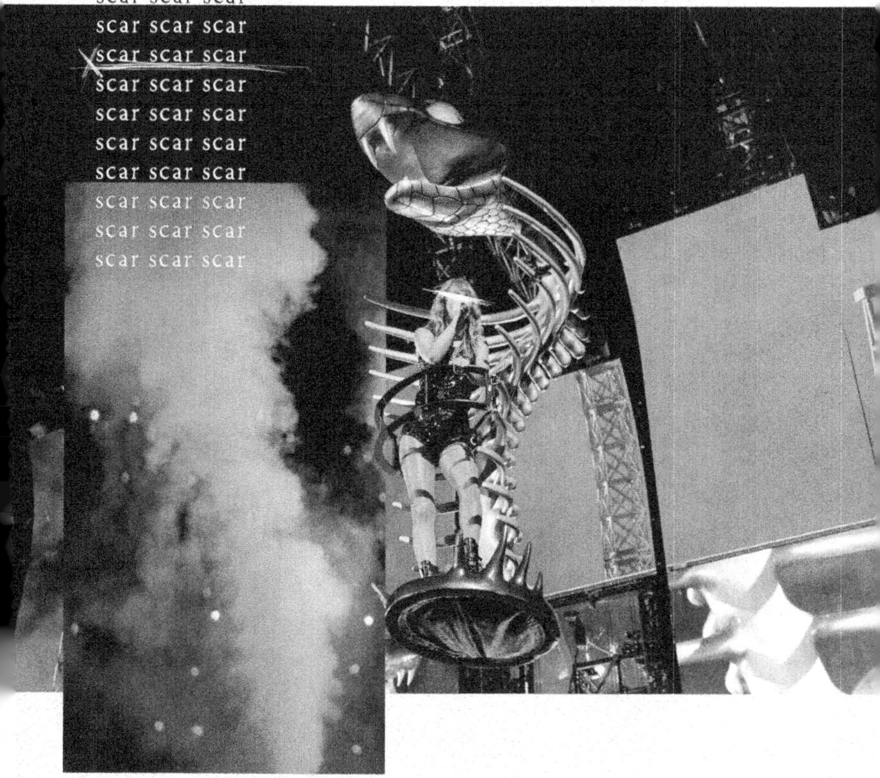

i did my best to suck out the poison,
cleaning my wounds
and washing away the dark ink
that ruined all our picture-perfect memories,
but there will always be stains
left to remind me
of the creature i became
when i let the bitterness spread.

i am trying
to be grateful
for your abandonment
because that lonely road
led me to a new adventure
where i found my secret power
— *"writer in the dark"*

I WILL ALWAYS
BE A CREATURE
OF BITTERNESS

you wouldn't recognize me
if you came back
    — "somebody that you used to know"

you never knew me anyway
you never knew me anyway
you never knew me anyway
you never knew me anyway
you never knew me anyway

a new dawn rose
after the long winter,
and i struck a match
deep within my heart
until the sparks
warmed my body
and i finally realized
who i could grow to be.
— *changed for good*

we don't need crystals
or tarot cards
because our magic
comes from something purer
— *witches of grace*

WITCH
WITCH

WITCH WITCH
WITCH WITCH WITCH
WITCH
WITCH WITCH
WITCH WITCH
WITCH WITCH
WITCH WITCH WITCH
WITCH WITCH WITCH
WITCH

the dark battles the light
in a true war of the worlds,
and yet the republic still dwells
on the battle of man.

the rulers cry
"WITCH!"
but they fail to see the infection
consuming their minds.

and so the witches have become soldiers,
fighting the beasts within themselves
while also battling the hatred
that pollutes their world.

even if the devil poisoned their cup,
they are still responsible
for their malevolence.
— *choose compassion*

why is it so difficult to be kind?

LIGHT UP
LIGHT UP
LIGHT UP
LIGHT UP

we alone must make the decision
to light up the darkness
and embrace our destinies
as shooting stars.
— *timshel ii*

every day i walk the line
between who i was
and who i am becoming,
forever fated to fall
into the same habits
that once chained me,
and sometimes i fear
my past will swallow me whole.

MY PAST IS DEVOURING ME

IS THIS
WHAT DROWING
FEELS LIKE?

your side effects
have lingered
longer than i ever thought
possible
— when will i finally be clean?

five years ago
today
the long lost lady asked me
to be in her wedding

five years ago
today
was the last time
i ever saw her
— *december 22, 2013*

i always
think about December

her dragon keeps haunting me
even after a decade,
and sometimes i wonder
if she ever became human again.

does she still hoard her gold?
does she still collect allies?
does she ever regret her skeletons?
does she ever think about me?
— *changed for good ii*

~~maybe~~ maybe you'll
always be a collector

238

I am okay on my own

maybe years from now
when you're married
and i'm okay on my own,
we'll cross paths,
and i'll smile at you
and actually mean it.
— *my hope for both of you*

i have buried my *grudges*
deep inside my soul,
and i hope that i can move on
if i cannot see them taunting me.

but like any time capsule,
i know that there will come a day
when i dig them up one last time
to celebrate the person i used to be.

239

once upon a time you called me *wicked*,
so i donned a black cloak
and embraced my title
until i watched my skin turn green.

green for eternity.
green for peace.
green for naivety.
green for renewal.

but after a lifetime
of shooing people away like flies,
i found myself
alone.

so i joined the rebels,
and i learned how to wield my magic.
i let the light wash away
a hundred thousand mistakes.

and now i see
we all have wickedness
hidden inside us.
but we have goodness too.

green

give us the freedom we are owed

the tyrants made claims
we were traitors and villains and thieves,
and soon the world turned against us,
believing those vicious lies.

our so-called "greed"
was nothing more than a cry for help.
we only wanted the freedoms we were owed,
but to the ears of royalty it sounded like stealing.

together we had power they did not,
and though we were accused, we still rallied.
and so we plotted
to steal our world back.

our greatest weapon
against the blackness within
is finding the ones
who truly see the light in us

isn't it
strange how people you've never met
can shape you
into who you're supposed to be?
— *delicate strangers*

DELICATE

i'll come back to you

we always find our way back to each other,
even after months apart,
even after miles away,
and i wonder if you missed me
as much as i missed you.
— *the constant*

i have stopped fearing
bitter feuds and hostile fallouts
because i know at our core,
you understand me
more than the other two ever did.
— *third time's the charm*

I will
always
fight for
you

244

our friendship manifests in milkshakes and mixtapes,
in soon-to-be-forgotten jokes and not-so-awkward silences.
sometimes we sit together in separate worlds,
connected by a single thread of shared memory.
in your smile, i see a life well-lived.
in your laugh, i hear a thousand symphonies.
you are the melody that always brings me back
to small town reminders
of the kind of teenager i wish i could've been.

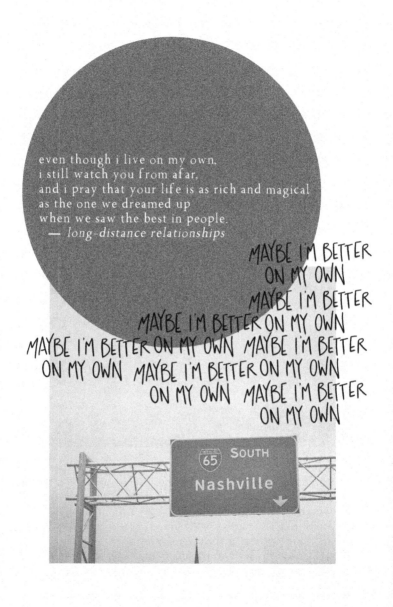

even though i live on my own,
i still watch you from afar,
and i pray that your life is as rich and magical
as the one we dreamed up
when we saw the best in people.
— *long-distance relationships*

MAYBE I'M BETTER ON MY OWN
MAYBE I'M BETTER
MAYBE I'M BETTER ON MY OWN
MAYBE I'M BETTER ON MY OWN MAYBE I'M BETTER
ON MY OWN MAYBE I'M BETTER ON MY OWN
ON MY OWN MAYBE I'M BETTER
ON MY OWN

65 SOUTH

Nashville

flowers will bloom again

sometimes the devil reaches for you,
hades coming to take his persephone away,
and i have to let you go back to the land of the dead.

it's been years since you first went under,
but i know the blue will always torment you,
no matter what i do.

so even though i can't save you from your own mind,
i promise to always welcome you home
whenever the _flowers_ sprout around you again.

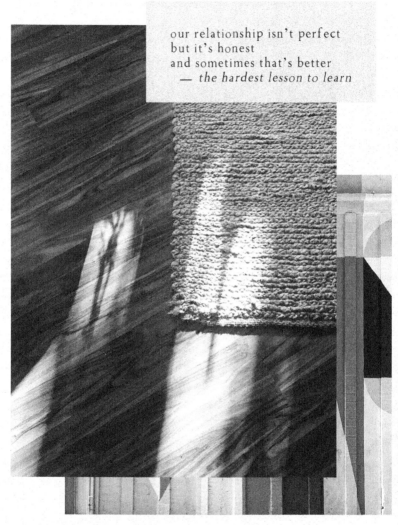

our relationship isn't perfect
but it's honest
and sometimes that's better
— *the hardest lesson to learn*

we must find people who contrast us
and challenge us to change,
for it is in that contrast
that we can learn and grow
and become our truest selves.
— *static people lead to static lives*

for once i did not
mention her name
when you said
something
that reminded me of her
— *"i'm ready to move on"*

now i only
see you in
the rearview

i don't miss her at all

missing you
hurts more
than losing her ever did
— *freedom*

there are worse things
than being alone
in a world as marvelous and vast
as this one

— *single & satisfied*

twilight grows longer
as we watch the commanders dismantle
our crumbling foundation.

the insurgents gather their power
and call on the sun
to pierce the black night.

though the people continue to cry out,
we grip our sisters and brothers
to summon the magic in our veins.

since our power protects us,
we must fight for those who cannot.
we must use our voices.
    — *for the ones who cannot speak*

join the rebellion

during our months apart,
my sorceress and i focus our strength outward,
on the witches we left behind.

as our crumbling world begins to take precedence,
we no longer fixate our lives
on a fragile kernel of fairytale friendship.

instead of prioritizing our crowns,
we each join the rebellion,
marching into a battle we never thought we'd fight.

our war is not with the skeletons in our closets
or the wickedness in our veins,
but with the black hate that has encompassed our kingdom.
— *something's changed this time*

choose empathy

swap your apathy for empathy
— *how to combat viciousness*

when the commanders on their thrones
could no longer corrupt me with their poison,
the devil began to attack my mind from within.

those creatures of the night that i had once vanquished
returned with an army of dark thoughts and deadly lies,
and they begged me to hate myself.

each silent sentinel of solitude sank its teeth into my thoughts
at the devil's command, forging a new reality
where i forgot my magic and yielded to the void.

SILENT
SENTINELS
OF
SOLITUDE

the blue manifests
in silence,
slowly filling me to the brim
until it overflows.

that quiet numbness awakens
with a monstrous appetite,
after months of sleeping,
ready to devour me whole.

so i fight it.
                  i treat it.
i whisper to it at night
to *please just leave me alone*
but it rages on.
  — *steady waters*

blue

darkness
~~dark~~
is a mountain

sometimes the darkness inside me feels like a mountain,
and i am being forced to climb to the top
while the earth crumbles underneath my feet.

how am i supposed to fight the blue
when there is black
bleeding into every corner of our universe?

i have heard the cries
of a hundred voices
demanding change,
weeping for freedom,
raging for justice,
but they are silenced
by a few old men
coughing on their thrones.

the screams grow louder.
— *WHEN WILL THE TYRANTS BURN*

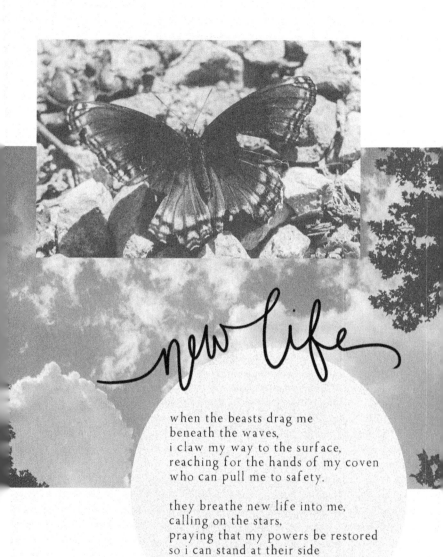

new life

when the beasts drag me
beneath the waves,
i claw my way to the surface,
reaching for the hands of my coven
who can pull me to safety.

they breathe new life into me,
calling on the stars,
praying that my powers be restored
so i can stand at their side
in the battle against the night.

our land has been overrun
by wolves in sheep's clothing,
but the dogs insist
that their beacon shines bright.

they spit excuses
and convince their spouses
that they answer to a higher power,
even as they worship themselves.

so they send their soldiers
to cut down the next generation,
silencing the young voices of truth
who long to burn their republic to the ground.
    — *strength in numbers*

after lifetimes of persisting,
the witches fought back
and licked the flames
that crawled up their arms.
they prayed for pain,
reveling in that fiery furnace,
so their daughters would be free.

let's remake the world

we can overcome
the acrimony of kings
by unlearning their rules
and cheating their games.

through self-love and kindness
our world will be remade,
and we'll find a new beginning
where everyone is loved the same.

light

though darkness tries to overwhelm us
and drown us in the sorrows of man,
we must not let it
dim the brightness of our souls.
— *i choose light*

for so many years i looked to you
to make sure you were still breathing,
but now i look to you as *the beacon*,
a lantern on my path when i'm stumbling
through the darkest part of the forest.
i know you are not perfect,
i know you are not my savior,
i know you are not the sorceress of my dreams,
but you are still the person i count on
to fight by my side.
  — *"out of the woods"*

i have to save myself first
before i can save anyone else
— the oxygen mask theory

i used to think i was running
from her ghost
but now i see that i'm sprinting
towards my destiny

running towards me

LET GO IT'S TIME
LET GO IT'S TIME TO LET GO
IT'S TIME TO LET GO IT'S TIME
IT'S TIME TO LET GO IT'S TIME
TO LET GO IT'S TIME TO LET GO
IT'S TIME TO LET GO

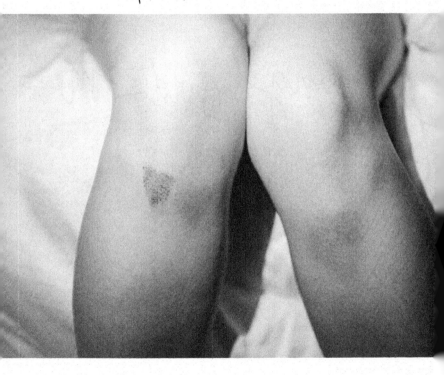

does she ever wonder
what happened to me?
— *all that remains*

all my old photographs
illustrate the lies
i told myself
when i was young.

i used to linger on minuscule details:
the greasy strands of a bad haircut,
the ever-increasing numbers on a scale,
the blotchy skin of a teenager.

but as i look back on who i was
and take in the forgotten moments,
i see through the lens of my mother
and i truly do not recognize myself.

i see a girl who was unburdened,
who laughed like the sun
and loved like a shooting star,
a girl who was imperfectly perfect.

i see myself,
but i do not see the me i remember.
— *black holes of my youth*

perfectly imperfect

i attack the worst parts of myself,
confronting the vicious creatures
i have allowed to live inside me,
and though my inner demons try
to overtake my tattered soul,
i will not let them win.

deep within my heart,
a fire is blossoming.
so i open myself up,
praying once more
that i am strong enough
to withstand the flames.

I AM
STRONG
ENOUGH

SELF-IMAGE

the secret
to all my power
is that i am no longer ashamed
of my reflection.
— *self-image*

i tossed her old letters
into a garbage bag
as casually as the remnants
of the dinner i had last night
and that's when i realized
she was fading
and i was shining
— *too self-oriented to remember you*

now when people mention her,
i do not bring up our past
because it does not belong to me,
but rather the person i used to be.
— *lost & found*

all the
people you
used to be
are rooting
for you

dear me,

no one can love you like you can love yourself
because no one knows you like you do.
so do not forget about your first soul-mate,
your truest love,
the one who will always be there,
and remember to nurture
the glimmer inside you.

— *self-care is not selfish*

i define my life
on my terms
on my time
on my own plane of existence
and no one
can take that away
from me
not even the republic

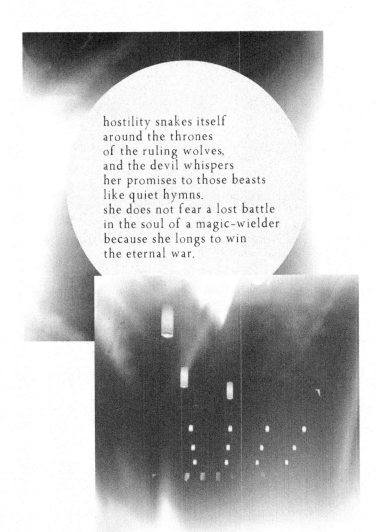

hostility snakes itself
around the thrones
of the ruling wolves,
and the devil whispers
her promises to those beasts
like quiet hymns.
she does not fear a lost battle
in the soul of a magic-wielder
because she longs to win
the eternal war.

~~the~~ the eternal war

I worship myself

it has taken years
for me to unlearn who i was for her,
to dislodge the cheap shots,
to sew up the torn shreds of trust,
to worship myself,
but i accomplished what she did not.
— i have learned how to be on my own

i'm so sick
of everyone telling me
that i need to find
my soul mate
— *plot twist: i'm my own soul-mate*

with a newfound strength in my core,
i finally join the ranks of the rebel soldiers,
all the while, conjuring weapons out of words.
in the distance, i see a cloud of dark smoke
advancing like a wolf across the land.
but no matter what's to come,
no matter what darkness the devil calls,
i must pay the debt i owe
to a people who will always deserve better.
i must use my voice
to rally our rebellion from the rooftops.
— *"salute"*

lace up your boots

first, they attack the children,
tearing them from the arms of their mothers
and locking them in cages
like rabid animals.

we let them.

then, the commanders burn the truth,
convincing us to build a barricade
to quarantine the outside world
where disease runs rampant.

we let them.

there is no final straw
because every wicked decree
breaks our backs
and we can only watch in terror.

we let them.

DO NOT LET THEM WIN.

so we must fight
against our apathy
and embrace our fates as world-changers.

no one else will stand up for the innocent.
no one else will fight for justice.
no one else will save our kingdom.
 — *though they give us trials, we will not cower*

no matter how loud we scream,
the nobility see our disobedience
as a teenage tantrum,
selfishly crying for justice
that doesn't exist in their picture-perfect world.

these binary beings embrace the throne
as it vows to enforce a world of black and white,
so long as the royals remain
in their pyramids of gold,
and no one disturbs their peace.

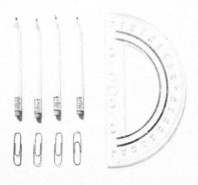

PICTURE PERFECT

they try to chain us,
to trap us in their laws,
but we resist
until we are strong enough
to escape their cells
and climb their fences.
we send shockwaves through loopholes,
using their own power against them
until they lose control of the people.
and though we cannot yet overcome them,
we do not back down.
  — *VOTE*

VOTE VOTE VOTE VOTE
VOTE VOTE VOTE VOTE VOTE
VOTE VOTE VOTE VOTE VOTE
VOTE VOTE VOTE VOTE VOTE
TE VOTE VOTE VOTE VOTE
VOTE VOTE VOTE

since they can no longer burn us,
the men try to silence our voices
and mute our resistance
until it fades away to indifference.
— *too little, too late*

you cannot
silence us

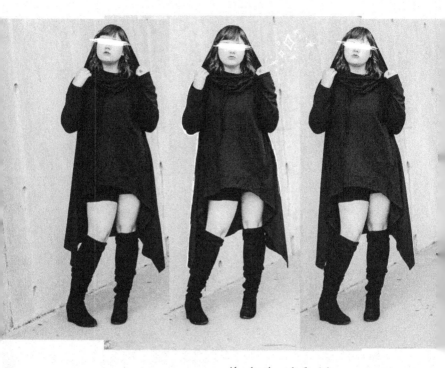

as i prepare to walk the battlefield,
i see an army of diversity
pushing against the midnight smoke
with conjurers and magic-wielders,
angels and enchantresses,
and one particularly powerful sorceress.

each smear of make-up and stroke of confidence
fuels my insurgence as i armor myself
to defend goodness and justice and truth,
and when i look beside me,
i see all the people who ever came to my aid,
offering up their power for all who seek sanctuary.

sometimes
    it is better to die
        in a blaze of light
      than to continue to live
        in suffocating darkness

light is coming

what DEMOCRACY looks like

i walk into battle
with red lips and black boots,
joining hands with my siblings
so we can shine like supernovas.
our union sends shockwaves
through the walls of glass
that surround our fragile homeland,
and we wait for the empire to collapse.
— *this is what democracy looks like*

the smallest fractures
e x p l o d e
into
the largest avalanches

but sometimes even avalanches
take
their
time
to
f
a
l
l

there is no grand conflict,
no one-on-one combat,
no fight to the death.
we do not open fire
on the thrones of the wicked
or murder the kings in their beds
because we will not stoop
to their level.
so we fight for little victories
and small changes
that will one day cascade
into something bigger.
— *we must fly higher*

even if we win the battle,
we may never win the war
until we can change the hearts
of those who sit on their self-appointed thrones.

epilogue

the fight continues
as the commanders rally their armies
and desolation preys on the weak.
fear creeps through the land
setting cities ablaze
until even the rebels doubt
themselves.

months waste away
and the resistance wanes,
slowly forgetting their fight
as if they have already been overcome.

but wickedness cannot conquer goodness
just as hate cannot vanquish love,
and even though the flame of hope flickers,
it cannot be extinguished.

so the magic-wielders must rise
and remember their stories.
they must fight for those who cannot
even when the fight hurts
even when the battle is lost
because even the darkest nights
yield to dawn.

remember your story

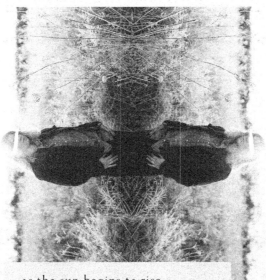

as the sun begins to rise,
i see a glimmer
of what the world could be,
where the witches become more
than their man-made labels,
and their children run free
without care or worry.
because even though a war rages,
we hold a weapon inside of us.
— *hope*

someday the antidote will come
to end the poison,
the infection,
the bad blood,
and we will be *ready for it*.

i am my own
happily ever after
   — *but this is not the end*

~~THE END~~

acknowledgements

to god - for countless blessings and infinite grace.

to taylor swift - who taught me to be fearless and speak now.

to sarah j. maas - who helped me heal the darkness inside myself.

to the beta fish - manda, hailee, laura, liv, katie, emily m, jacque, hannah, kat, ryan, summer, dylan, anne, olivia, surega, emily l, courtney w, robby, jess, gabby, nicole, courtney h - I cannot tell you how grateful I am to each of you for taking the time out of your life to critique the early versions of this narrative. I showed you my heart, and you didn't run from it. Thank you for pushing me to make this work better and for listening to my story.

to my author supporters - amanda lovelace, sasha alsberg, sophia elaine hanson - Thank you for using your words to help this little book go far! I admire all of you greatly and your kind blurbs mean the world to me.

to my art contributors - margot groner, aurora phommalysack, sophia maxwell - Thank you for your contributions to this collection! Your art always wows me and I'm so glad it could be included with my poems!

to mom & dad - Thank you for encouraging me to explore my creative potential and for always supporting me - even when I do crazy things like drive cross-country or fly to New York to see broadway shows. I value your wisdom, your patience, your generosity, and above all, your love. I am so blessed to have you in my life, and I hope you know how much I love and adore you.

SPEAK NOW SPEAK NOW SPEAK NOW
SPEAK NOW SPEAK NOW SPEAK NOW

long live

to jon - The Ross to my Monica. No matter what happens, I will never stop trying to impress you in the hopes that you'll think I'm cool. You always amaze me with your intelligence, humor, and wisdom. Even when we don't agree or get along, I know we have a bond that no one else will understand - I couldn't have asked for a better brother.

to my extended family - I'm so thankful that I got to grow up with such a vibrant group of people. You all taught me about kindness and true love, and I will never stop admiring you. Thank you for the life lessons, the old stories, and the never-ending bad jokes. You are some of the most caring and genuine people in my life, and I love you dearly.

to hannah zygmunt - My true sister. I could write a whole other poetry collection about my friendship and sisterhood with you, and I feel truly blessed to have known you since I was born. You've seen me through the good, the bad, and the ugly and you are such a light to me. Even though I never technically chose you, I will always love you because you are my family. Long live!

to laura gruszka - My parabatai. There are no words to acknowledge your role in my life and in this collection. I still cannot believe that you printed out all 50+ pages of the first draft to write out your exact critiques. Thank you for listening to my weird rants and reading my obsessive text messages and for always believing in me, even when I don't believe in myself. Thank you for being a part of my forget-me-nots and marigolds.

28

to **hailee bartz** - My twin. You have been so enthusiastic about my writing and my passions, and I don't know what I did to deserve you in my life. I am always in awe of your kind heart, your lively spirit, and your ridiculous sense of humor, and I'm obsessed with you. There's no one I'd rather dance in the rain with!!

to amy schuh - My North Star. You have been with me from day one, and I can never thank you enough for sticking with me even when I retreat into myself - you always pull me back to the world of the living. You're stronger than you know, and your friendship means everything to me. The odds are always in your favor, even when you don't think so!

to jacque jordan - My partner-in-crime. Your talent will always amaze me, and I'm so thankful that God pushed us together because we are truly the dream team. You are going to do great things, and I'm so happy I get to watch you share your gifts with the world. No one gets me quite like you, and I cherish every late-night pre-shower talk!

to katie strange - My other, slightly more extroverted half. I never would have imagined that you'd become so important to me when I first saw you on YouTube, but I feel incredibly grateful that we got the opportunity to become real life friends. You make me feel seen even when I'm trying to hide, and I really appreciate all the ways you love me. Thank you for accepting me and my weird Type Five quirks!

OH MY GOD! IT'S JENNA CLARKE!!

to emily minarik - My #1 fan. Even though you can sometimes be a thorn in my side, I am so blessed to have you standing next to me (even with a semi-broken foot). You break me out of my comfort zone and force me to do things that make me grow. Thank you for putting up with my stubbornness and for not giving up on me!

to amanda lovelace - You are the first person who really pushed me to write down my story in poetry, and it's because of your own writing that I even considered doing so in the first place. Not only are you incredibly talented, but you're also supportive and honest and kind, and I am so thankful I decided to follow you on Tumblr all those years ago. You're the main reason this collection even exists!

thank you

to greg karas - It's been 15 years since I was in your class, but I still hold you responsible for giving me my love of words. I never really believed it was possible that I'd publish a book, but I think you always knew. Thank you for encouraging me to seek out magical worlds and for always making me smile. Hopefully this story lives up to your standards!

to andi stepnik - Thank you for forcing me to do better even when it was difficult. You taught me about a new way to see the world, and I will never be able to thank you enough for that. Your classes always kicked my ass, but looking back I am grateful for them because they made me grow. Thank you for all the ways you support the people around you - I really appreciate you!

to christy ridings - I never thought I'd have a mentor, but you have become that person for me. You ask me the hard questions and you know when to break me out of my shell. Thank you for always seeing the best in me and for pushing me to be the person God called me to be. You've helped me in more ways than you know!

to my forgotten friends - *allison tunstall, ashleigh schneider, danielle weiler, faith briggs, hannah albers, hannah zygmunt, jessalyn ayers, lexie bluhm, natalie wirsing, stephanie baxter-ivey, taylor williams, tess galbiati, victoria perez* - High school was a long time ago now, but I will always remember the girls who grew up with me. Some of you knew me when I was tiny, some of you I only have known for a short part of my life, but all of you loved me even when I thought I was invisible. You noticed me when I disappeared behind my books and my guitar, and I will always thank you for that.

VHS CLASS of 2013

to my bookternet family - *aaron brignac, alexandra ling, aly konkel, amanda koger, amanda lovelace, angus woodiwiss, ariel bissett, arthur lembo, ashley nuckles, ash nguyen, ben alderson, brigitte cormier, caden sage, caitlin vanasse, camila rodríguez laureano, cambria evans, carmen seda, carolyn king, catriona feeney, chami rupasinghe, christina marie, christina nilsson, christine riccio, cody corall, courtney wells, cyrus parker, dave connis, dylan calvert, elisabeth olsen, ellias hoang, emma giordano, emma green, emily luedloff, emily minarik, erin cleary, gabriela pop, gio navas, hailee bartz, hailey leblanc, hannah azerang, heather davis, jay gaunt, j.d. netto, jeremy & jeffrey west, jess sheppard, jesse george, jesy elyse, jillian coffey, jordan hickey, kaitlyn foster, kamalia hasni, kat o'keeffe, kathleen graham, katie strange, kayla rayne, kayley hyde, kav lakshmi, kevin kelly, kirstyn hippe, kristina horner, laura donohue, laure dombrecht, lauren rathjens, lindsay cummings, lindsay & tiffany keiler, lily gaines, liv páez, liz vallish, marie grace sterling, maureen graham, max dunn, meagan precourt, michael d'angelo, mike ploetz, mónica pradilla, monica watson, monica white, natasha polis, paige firth, payton lewis, rayna liddell, regan perusse, reggie smith, robby weber, rowan drury, sabrina handal, sandy lu, sanaa storia, sarawithoutanh, sasha alsberg, soph o solano, sophia elaine hanson, sophia lee, taylor friedlander, taylor joy stanley, tiernan bertrand-essington, trina ruck, tzivi kleinbart, whitney atkinson, wil hallstrom, zoë herdt & so many more -* I never thought I would have friends who live all around the globe, but each of you mean so much to me. You have given me so much confidence, and you always make me feel like I'm one of the cool kids. You all inspire me every single day, and I am amazed by your kindness and sincerity. This one's for you!

— BE YOUR OWN HAPPY ENDING —

to my selfless sisterhood - *abi inglis, allison hardee, amy schuh, emily ryder, emily dempsey, frances praet, grace watson, haile-montana di tieri, jacque jordan, janie townsend, kat waggaman, laura tileston, marci greene, maxine bouldin, monica smith, nicollette barreras, sally-ann jones, sarah beth jones, sierra griffin* - When I went to college, I always hoped I would find a group of lifelong friends, but I never imagined I would join a fake sorority full of real sisters. Every time I'm with you, I feel the love of God, and I hope one day I can be even half as selfless and generous as y'all. *Makka Sakka Pi* will always live on in our hearts, and I am so grateful to have you as a part of my story.

ΜΣΠ

to my followers - For anyone who has ever subscribed or liked or followed or commented on any of the weird content I post, thank you. I make most of my art for me, but to know that there are people out there who care about me and enjoy seeing what I create...that brings me a joy I cannot explain. You are the reason why I decided to share this book with the world. Don't let anyone tell you that you can't do something because you are more powerful and strong than you know. Be your own happy ending!

to the witches who battle the tyrants - I stand with you & I hope you find strength in my words.

to those who inspired this work - I did not write this out of malice, but rather because I needed closure from both of you. For a long time I felt incredibly bitter about how our relationships ended, but I never found a good way to explore my feelings - the good ones and the bad ones. This collection has allowed me to find peace, and I hope one day we can truly be happy for each other and the lives we've created in each other's absence. Above all, I know you both changed me for good, and for that I am grateful.

about the author

Jenna

Jenna Clare is a writer and photographer who has spent
the last decade putting various types of art on the internet.
After growing up in Northwest Indiana, she moved to
Nashville, TN to study Audio & Video Production at
Belmont University where she got a Bachelor of Science
degree. Although she still has a day job, Jenna runs her
own freelance photography business as well as a
semi-successful YouTube channel where she talks about
books, music, and her life. When she isn't scrolling
through social media, you can find her listening to Taylor
Swift songs, taking photos of her friends, or
binge-watching tv shows.

instagram: @jennaclarek
twitter: @jennaclarek
website: http://jennaclarek.com

Made in the USA
Columbia, SC
30 December 2020

30079716R00166